Grizzly Bears
Saving the Silvertip

by Jacqueline Dembar Greene

Consultant: Kerry Gunther
Bear Management Office
Yellowstone National Park

BEARPORT PUBLISHING

New York, New York

Credits

Cover and Title Page, © franzfoto.com/Alamy; 4, © Andy Rouse/The Image Bank/Getty Images; 5, © Craighead Collection; 7, © Breck P. Kent/Animals Animals-Earth Scenes; 8, Remington Arms Company; 9, © Whyte Museum of the Canadian Rockies, V263/NA-2847, Archives Society of Alberta, Title: 271. A day's hunt, 3 grizzlies. A.O. Wheeler & T.G. Longstaff, Wheeler's Bugaboo Expedition, Title: Byron Harmon Dates: 1910; 10, © Lynn Stone/Animals Animals-Earth Scenes; 11, © age fotostock/SuperStock; 12, © Stouffer Productions/Animals Animals-Earth Scenes; 13, © Craighead Collection; 14, © Yellowstone National Park, US Department of the Interior; 15, © Don Skillman/Animals Animals-Earth Scenes; 16, © Carl & Ann Purcell/Corbis; 17, © Daniel J. Cox/Corbis; 18, © age fotostock/SuperStock; 19, © Craighead Collection; 20, © Steve Winter/National Geographic Image Collection; 21, © Jean Capps, Photographer; 23, © age fotostock/SuperStock; 24, © Derek Reich/Zööprax Productions; 25, © Scott Sine/Courtesy of Wind River Bear Institute; 26, © Yellowstone National Park, US Department of the Interior; 27, © Shattil & Rozinski/naturepl.com; 28, © S. Michael Bisceglie/Animals Animals-Earth Scenes; 29T, © Paul Nicklen/National Geographic Image Collection; 29B, © Vova Pomortzeff/Shutterstock; 31, © Stephen Finn/Shutterstock.

Publisher: Kenn Goin
Senior Editor: Lisa Wiseman
Creative Director: Spencer Brinker
Photo Researcher: Beaura Ringrose
Cover Design: Dawn Beard Creative

Library of Congress Cataloging-in-Publication Data

Greene, Jacqueline Dembar.
 Grizzly bears : saving the silvertip / by Jacqueline Dembar Greene.
   p. cm. — (America's animal comebacks)
 Includes bibliographical references and index.
 ISBN-13: 978-1-59716-533-4 (library binding)
 ISBN-10: 1-59716-533-6 (library binding)
 1. Grizzly bear—Conservation—West (U.S.)—Juvenile literature. 2. Rare mammals—West (U.S.)—Juvenile literature. I. Title.

QL737.C27.G7395 2008
599.784—dc22

                              2007012606

For more information, write to Bearport Publishing Company, Inc., 101 Fifth Avenue, Suite 6R, New York, New York 10003. Printed in the United States of America.

10 9 8 7 6 5 4 3 2 1

Contents

Tracking the Grizzly

It was 1960, and **biologists** John and Frank Craighead had just **tagged** a sleeping grizzly bear's ear when they heard a loud growl. The bear roared awake. The **tranquilizer** they had given the animal must have worn off too quickly! The Craighead brothers raced toward their car as the bear chased them. They jumped in and watched as the angry animal smashed a dent in one of the doors. Luckily, they were able to safely drive away.

Grizzly bears live in North America. They are one of the largest mammals on the continent.

The Craighead brothers were studying grizzly bears in Yellowstone **National Park**. During their 12 years of work there, they developed **radio collars**. The collars let them track the bears' movements and learn more about them.

Through their research, the brothers discovered something shocking. Grizzly bears were dying out. Could anything be done to save them?

Twin brothers John and Frank Craighead tranquilized and put a radio collar around this grizzly's neck. They checked its age, weight, and health.

Grizzlies have silver-tipped fur.
They are often called silvertips.

Shrinking Habitat

Grizzlies weren't always in danger. In the early 1700s, about 100,000 roamed the western part of North America. They lived between the Mississippi River and the Pacific Ocean. They could also be found as far north as Alaska and Canada and as far south as Mexico.

Where grizzly bears lived in North America before 1850
Yellowstone National Park

During the 1800s, **pioneers** moved west. Settlers cleared the land to build homes and plant crops. Lumber companies cut down forests. Oil companies drilled deep into the ground. All this construction was not good for silvertips. The land where they lived was being destroyed. Their **habitat** was shrinking.

When forests are cut down, bears lose the protection of wooded areas. They also lose food that comes from trees and bushes, such as nuts and berries.

The Killing Begins

As their habitat shrank, silvertips found it harder to find food. Occasionally, the hungry bears attacked **livestock**, such as sheep and cattle. To protect their animals, ranchers shot the big bears on sight.

Silvertips also faced another threat—hunting. Some people killed the bears because they thought the animals were dangerous. Others killed them for their fur, which could be sold for a lot of money.

This ad encouraged people, in the 1800s and early 1900s, to buy rifles to protect themselves from bears.

Between 1871 and 1872, hunters killed at least 750 silvertips in a small area that is now Saskatchewan, Canada.

Habitat loss and hunting took a toll on the grizzly **population**. By 1935, they had disappeared from most of North America. Only a few hundred bears were left in Montana, Idaho, and Wyoming. More silvertips survived in Alaska and Canada, where there was still plenty of open land.

These two hunters shot three silvertips in one day.

Hungry Bears

When the Craighead brothers began their study in Yellowstone National Park in 1959, scientists knew little about silvertips. The Craigheads wanted to learn about the bears' bodies, what they ate, and how they lived.

Meadow grass, called sedge, makes up a big part of a grizzly's diet.

The Craigheads followed the bears that they put radio collars on. The brothers discovered that grizzlies eat a lot—90 pounds (41 kg) of food a day. They need to store up plenty of fat for winter, when they **hibernate**.

The brothers also found that silvertips eat different foods in different seasons. In spring, they depend on meadow grass and **bulbs**. Then each summer, they travel to rivers to catch salmon. In fall, they gobble forest berries and nuts.

One grizzly can eat 200,000 berries in one day!

Grizzlies love fishing for salmon. The bears fish in different ways. Some might swat a fish with their paws, while others catch the fish in their mouths.

More Food Means More Bears

The radio collars proved to be a very important part of the Craigheads' study. The beeps from the collars led them to the bears' **dens**. They were able to see how the bears spent the cold months of winter.

The collars also allowed the Craigheads to learn more about grizzly **cubs**. They were able to follow them and keep track of their weight and health.

Each fall most grizzly bears dig a new den. Some bears might use their dens from the year before.

The brothers discovered that well-fed female bears **mate** when they are young. They give birth to a **litter** of cubs once every three years. However, females without a good supply of rich food mate much later in life. These bears have just one cub, or sometimes none. Less food means fewer cubs. Fewer cubs mean a smaller grizzly population.

Frank Craighead crawls through a narrow opening of a grizzly's den.

Cubs that don't get enough food will not live long. Up to half of all grizzly cubs die before they are two years old.

The Dumps

Grizzlies inside Yellowstone, and those in its surrounding areas, were well fed. They had a constant food source. Campers left tons of garbage behind. Huge dumps filled up with leftover food and trash. Grizzlies smelled the food and came to the dumps for an easy meal.

A bear in Yellowstone eating food from a dump

Yellowstone National Park stretches into parts of Wyoming, Montana, and Idaho.

The dumps were located near campsites. When the bears came to get the food, it often caused problems. Between 1931 and 1969, there were about 48 bear attacks against campers each year. Grizzlies were also known for causing damage to campers' property. In 1967, park officials decided that they needed to reduce the number of these incidents. They decided to close the dumps.

Brown bears and grizzly bears in other parks in North America also eat from garbage dumps.

More Bear Deaths

The Craigheads were not happy with the plan to close the dumps. They felt that the three biggest dumps were being closed too quickly and close together. They wanted the bears to have more time to get used to finding food from other places. Officials, however, decided to go ahead with their plan.

This sign, in Glacier National Park in Montana, warns campers and hikers not to feed or go near bears.

Bear Country

All Wildlife Is Dangerous
Do Not Approach Or Feed

When the dumps closed, park rangers planned to capture bears that entered a campground. Then they would free them miles (km) away. If the grizzlies returned, rangers would shoot them to protect campers. Between 1968 and 1973, park officials reported that they killed 52 grizzlies.

The Craigheads were upset that park officials did not listen to them. They decided to end their Yellowstone research in 1971.

Silvertips often stand upright. This helps them smell the location of people, animals, and food from great distances.

Though the Craigheads didn't agree with it, the park's plan was considered a success. Yellowstone now has about one bear attack per year as well as fewer reports of bears causing damage.

Save the Silvertip

Even though the Craigheads left Yellowstone, their work with grizzlies did not end. During their time in Yellowstone, John and Frank learned that silvertips need a lot of land to find food. However, people continued to build on land in the western United States where grizzlies lived. The grizzly habitat continued to shrink and the bears were still in danger of becoming **extinct**.

A mother grizzly and her cubs

To help save the bears' habitat, the brothers called for the government to create more protected areas such as Yellowstone. They also published their Yellowstone findings and wrote articles about the grizzlies. They hoped their studies would help the government take action.

Frank (left) and John in 1985

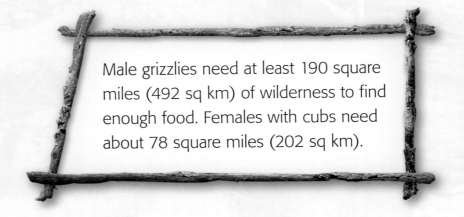

Male grizzlies need at least 190 square miles (492 sq km) of wilderness to find enough food. Females with cubs need about 78 square miles (202 sq km).

Taking Action

By 1975, only about 200 silvertips remained in Yellowstone. Less than 1,000 silvertips remained in the entire **lower United States**. As a result, the U.S. government finally took action. The bears were listed as **threatened** under the **Endangered Species** Act. People could no longer hunt or kill bears in most areas of the country.

Poachers continued to hunt bears illegally. Some poachers were caught and sent to prison. One poacher said he had shot 1,000 grizzlies.

Poachers sold bear hides, such as this one, for a lot of money.

The government also tried to protect the bears' habitat. It banned the building of roads in many areas where the bears lived. Logging and drilling for oil were also not allowed in large areas around Yellowstone.

Government scientists continued to study the bears, too. They looked for new ways to count the number of silvertips and to increase their population.

Poachers also sold grizzly bear paws. Some people used them to make Asian medicines.

A Grizzly Debate

Finally, under government protection, the number of grizzlies increased. By 2004, scientists **estimated** that between 500 and 600 bears lived in Yellowstone and its surrounding areas. There were about 50,000 found in Alaska and Canada.

Some people, however, weren't happy that the government was protecting the grizzlies. Companies wanted to be free to start new building and lumber projects. Others wanted to hunt the bears again.

☐ Where grizzly bears live in North America today

☐ Yellowstone National Park

In 2006, scientists sent a letter to the government. One of the signers was John Craighead, now 89 years old. The letter urged the government to keep grizzlies under protection. More letters came from other people supporting the big bear.

In March 2007, the government took the Yellowstone silvertips off the endangered species list. However, threatened grizzlies in other parts of the United States remain on the list.

Many groups, such as the National Wildlife Foundation, work hard to help save grizzly bears.

This group of grizzlies is fishing for their lunch.

Making New Tracks

Today, wildlife scientists are trying new methods to save bears from getting shot or caught and destroyed by people. In Montana, biologist Carrie Hunt trains dogs to teach grizzlies to stay away from humans. If a bear comes to a settled area, wildlife officers trap it. Hunt and her team then free the bear while the dogs bark and chase it back into the wilderness.

Carrie Hunt started her Wind River Bear Institute in Montana in 1996. Trained dogs like Tuffy teach grizzlies to avoid people.

Hunt wants grizzlies to remember the loud barking so they won't come back to the area. So far, her noisy plan has worked. Up to 300 bears in the United States and Canada have been saved. Other people throughout North America are using her plan, too.

Hunt uses Karelian bear dogs for her program. The dogs are from Finland and are used for hunting bears and elk.

This grizzly will be glad to have some peace and quiet.

What Else Can Be Done?

Grizzlies still need more help to increase their population. **Ecologists** believe creating new wilderness areas that are connected to one another can help. These areas would give grizzly bears a larger habitat in which to live and find food.

Radio collars developed by the Craigheads are still used today.

Teaching people about bear safety can help save people—and bears. National park rangers remind visitors to keep food in sealed containers so bears won't smell it. Yellowstone even has bear-proof garbage cans to keep the animals away. Hikers are told to make noise as they walk so they don't surprise the bears.

People once thought grizzlies were a threat. Yet it was humans who were threatening the bears. Today, thanks to the hard work of people like the Craigheads, the grizzlies now have a chance to survive.

Bear-proof food containers were tested in Denali National Park in Alaska. They lowered the amount of times bears got into hikers' food by almost 75 percent.

Grizzly Bear Facts

In 1973, Congress passed the Endangered Species Act. This law protects animals and plants that are in danger of dying out in the United States. Harmful activities, such as hunting, capturing, or collecting endangered species, are illegal under this act.

The grizzly bear was one of the first species listed under the Endangered Species Act. Grizzly bears in Yellowstone National Park were listed as a threatened species in 1975. Here are some other facts about the grizzly bear.

Population: North American population in 1700: **about 100,000**
Population in Alaska and Canada today: **about 50,000**
Population in the lower United States today: **about 1,000**

Weight
males: 400–800 pounds (181–363 kg); females: 350–400 pounds (159–181 kg)

Height
8–10 feet (2–3 m), from nose to tail

Fur Color
white, blond, cream, tan, brown, reddish brown, chocolate brown, or black; all fur is silver-tipped

Food
grasses, wildflowers, roots, berries, nuts, honey, insects, fish, clams, meat

Life Span
about 18 years; in some areas they can live into their late 20s

Habitat
Alaska, parts of Canada, Idaho, Montana, Wyoming, Washington

Other Bears in Danger

The grizzly bear is one kind of bear that's making a comeback by increasing its numbers. Other types of bears are also trying to make a comeback.

Polar Bears

- Polar bears live along the shores of the Arctic Ocean. Their creamy white fur keeps them warm, and helps them blend in with the snow and ice.

- Polar bears are in danger of disappearing due to loss of habitat. Many scientists believe their greatest danger is warmer temperatures and melting sea ice.

- Researchers are studying the effects of **global warming** on polar bears. They are looking for ways to save sea ice.

- People who illegally hunt polar bears are fined.

Sun Bears

- Sun bears live in the forests of Asia in Borneo, Burma, Thailand, and the Malay Peninsula. They are the smallest bears in the world.

- Sun bears are thought to be dying out. No one knows how many are left in the wild. Hunting, capturing, and loss of habitat are decreasing their numbers.

- Many countries have now banned the sale of bear parts. Scientists are breeding bears at some zoos to increase their population.

Glossary

biologists (bye-OL-uh-jists) scientists who study plants and animals

bulbs (BUHLBS) underground parts of plants

cubs (KUHBZ) baby bears

dens (DENZ) the homes of wild animals

ecologists (ee-KOL-uh-jists) people who study the relationships between plants, animals, and their environments

endangered (en-DAYN-jurd) in danger of dying out

estimated (ESS-ti-*mayt*-id) guessed an amount of something

extinct (ek-STINGKT) when a kind of plant or animal has died out; no more of its kind is living anywhere in the world

global warming (GLOHB-uhl WARM-ing) the warming of Earth's atmosphere and oceans

habitat (HAB-uh-*tat*) the place in nature where a plant or animal lives

hibernate (HYE-bur-nayt) to spend the winter in a deep sleep

litter (LIT-ur) a group of bears born at the same time to the same mother

livestock (LIVE-*stok*) animals such as sheep, chickens, and cows, that are raised on a farm or ranch

lower United States (LOH-ur yoo-NITE-id STATES) all U.S. states except Alaska and Hawaii

mate (MAYT) to come together to produce young

national park (NASH-uh-nuhl PARK) an area of land set aside by the government to protect the animals and plants that live there

pioneers (*pye*-uh-NEERZ) the first people to live in a new area

poachers (POHCH-urz) people who hunt or fish illegally

population (*pop*-yuh-LAY-shuhn) the total number of a kind of animal living in a place

radio collars (RAY-dee-oh KOL-urz) electronic devices placed around animals' necks that send out signals, allowing the animals to be tracked

species (SPEE-sheez) groups that animals are divided into, according to similar characteristics; members of the same species can have offspring together

tagged (TAGD) put a metal label on an animal in order to be able to identify it later on

threatened (THRET-uhnd) to be in immediate danger

tranquilizer (TRANG-kwuhl-*eyz*-ur) a drug that calms a person or animal, or puts them to sleep

Bibliography

Busch, Robert H. *The Grizzly Almanac.* Guilford, CT: The Lyons Press (2000).

Craighead, Jr., Frank C. *Track of the Grizzly.* San Francisco: Sierra Club Books (1979).

Hirschi, Ron. *Searching for Grizzlies.* Honesdale, PA: Boyds Mills Press (2005).

Read More

Gibbons, Gail. *Grizzly Bears.* New York: Holiday House (2003).

Klingel, Cynthia, and Robert B. Noyed. *Grizzly Bears.* Mankato: MN: The Child's World (2002).

Petersen, Shirley A. *Grizzlies and Other Bears.* Chicago: World Book, Inc. (2001).

Stone, Lynn M. *Grizzlies.* Minneapolis, MN: Carolrhoda (1993).

Learn More Online

To learn more about grizzly bears, visit
www.bearportpublishing.com/AnimalComebacks

Index

About the Author

Jacqueline Dembar Greene is an award-winning author of more than 30 fiction and nonfiction books and stories for young readers, including *The Triangle Shirtwaist Factory Fire* and *The 2001 World Trade Center Attack*. Some of her nonfiction books are illustrated with her original photographs. Learn more at www.jdgbooks.com.